Canada Close Up

Ontario

Adrianna Morganelli

Scholastic Canada Ltd.

Toronto New York London Auckland Sydney
Mexico City New Delhi Hong Kong Buenos Aires

Visual Credits

Cover: A.G.E. Foto Stock/First Light; p i: Frank Hudec/First Light; p. iii: A.G.E. Foto Stock/First Light; p. iv: Galyna Andrushko/Shutterstock Inc. (top left), Igor Grochev/Shutterstock Inc. (middle), Nguyen Thai/Shutterstock Inc. (top right); p. 2: Tootles/Shutterstock Inc.; p. 3: Henry Georgi/AllCanadaPhotos.com; p. 5: Alexandar Iotzov/Shutterstock Inc.; pp. 6-7: Pierre Guevremont/First Light; p. 8: Nialat/SnapVillage (bottom), Clarence W. Norris/Lone Pine Photo (middle); p. 9: Pavel Cheiko/Shutterstock Inc. (bottom and back cover), Philip Dalton/Alamy (top); p. 10: Bert Hoferichter/Alamy; p. 11: Thomas Kitchin/First Light (top), Sylvana Rega/Shutterstock Inc. (bottom); p. 12: Toronto Star/First Light; p. 13: North Wind/North Wind Picture Archives; p. 14: North Wind/North Wind Picture Archives; p. 15: Library and Archives Canada, Acc. No. 1989-401-1; p. 17: William Berczy, Thayendanegea (Joseph Brant), c. 1807 National Gallery of Canada, Ottawa; p. 18: North Wind/North Wind Picture Archives; pp. 19, 20: Government of Ontario Art Collection, Archives of Ontario; p. 21: The Print Collector/Alamy; p. 22: The Print Collector/Alamy; p. 23: Alan Marsh/First Light; p. 24: Ron Erwin/AllCanadaPhotos.com; p. 25: Thomson, Tom (Canadian, 1877 - 1917) *The West Wind*, winter 1916-1917, oil on canvas 120.7 x 137.9 cm ART GALLERY OF ONTARIO, TORONTO. Gift of the Canadian Club of Toronto, 1926 © 2008 Art Gallery of Ontario; p. 26: National Library of Canada NL-15557 (top), National Archives of Canada C-067337 (middle), Susanna Moodie, 1869. © Public Domain, National Library of Canada NL-15558 (bottom); p. 27: John T. Fowler/Alamy; p. 28: Vlad Ghiea/Shutterstock Inc.; p. 29: CP Photo/Aaron Harris (bottom), Toronto Star/First Light (top); p. 30: Paul A. Souders/CORBIS; pp. 30-31: Aron Brand/Shutterstock Inc.; p. 31: Foodfolio/Alamy (top), Foto Factory/Shutterstock Inc. (bottom); p. 32: Paul A. Souders/CORBIS; p. 34: Greg Taylor/Greg Taylor Photography (top), Dick Loek/Toronto Star (bottom); p. 35: Imagesource/First Light; p. 36: Jim Chernishenko (top); CP Photo/Bob Tymczyszyn (bottom); p. 37: Brian Summers/First Light; p. 39: CP Images/Kazuyoshi Ehara; p. 40: CP Photo/Kitchener-Waterloo Record-Staff; p. 41: CP Photo/Toronto Star-Tony Bock (top), Winston Fraser/Alamy (bottom); p. 42: The Print Collector/Alamy (top), World History Archive/Alamy (middle), Peter Mintz/First Light (bottom); p. 43: Jeff Goode/Toronto Star (top), Courtesy of the Dr. James Naismith Basketball Foundation (bottom).

www.scholastic.ca

Produced by Plan B Book Packagers
Editorial: Ellen Rodger
Design: Rosie Gowsell-Pattison
Special thanks to consultant and editor Terrance Cox, adjunct professor, Brock University; Jon Eben Field; Jim Chernishenko; and Colleen Beard and Sharon Janzen, Brock University Map Library.

Library and Archives Canada Cataloguing in Publication
Morganelli, Adrianna, 1979-
Ontario / Adrianna Morganelli.
(Canada close up)
ISBN 978-0-545-98904-6

1. Ontario--Juvenile literature. I. Title. II. Series: Canada close up (Toronto, Ont.)

FC3061.2.M67 2009   j971.3   C2008-906871-8

ISBN-10 0-545-98904-3

7 6 5 4   Printed in Singapore 46   14 15 16 17

Contents

Ontario's provincial gemstone is the amethyst.

Ontario's official flower is the white trillium.

CANADA

ARCTIC OCEAN

Russia

Alaska (U.S.A.)

Greenland (Denmark)

Iceland

Yukon

Northwest Territories

Nunavut

ATLANTIC OCEAN

British Columbia

Newfoundland and Labrador

Hudson Bay

PACIFIC OCEAN

Alberta

Saskatchewan

Manitoba

James Bay

Quebec

Prince Edward Island

Ontario

Nova Scotia

New Brunswick

Lake Huron

United States

Lake Superior

Lake Ontario

Lake Michigan

Lake Erie

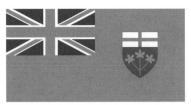

Welcome to Ontario!

Ontario is a vast and varied province of over one million square kilometres. It is so large that Italy, France and Germany could fit inside it with room to spare! More than thirteen million people from many different **ethnic** backgrounds live here.

Ontario is also a centre for manufacturing and for the entertainment industry. Its factories produce more than half of all the goods made in Canada. The province's capital, Toronto, has the second-highest number of theatres in North America.

Ontario's landscape is as diverse as its people. The Canadian Shield, Canada's largest rock formation, separates the north and the south. Forests, grassy lowlands and lakes cover the north while Ontario's south boasts rich farmland. Ontario is yours to discover!

Chapter 1
Shining Waters

Ontario means beautiful, or shining, waters in the Iroquoian language. And for good reason. More than nineteen per cent of Ontario's surface area is water. That's about one-third of the world's total fresh water supply!

There are more than 250,000 lakes in Ontario. Four of the five Great Lakes are located partly in Ontario. There are also countless streams and rivers.

Waterways were the province's original transportation routes. Using canoes, Aboriginal peoples travelled them for thousands of years. Later, the early European explorers used the same waterways to search for new lands and riches – long before any roads or modern highways were built.

Canals and byways

Today, the Great Lakes–St. Lawrence Seaway System is Ontario's main waterway. This network of six canals and nineteen locks allows ships to travel along the St. Lawrence River and through the Great Lakes. The system extends 3700 kilometres into the heart of North America.

The Welland Canal locks at St. Catharines move ships between Lake Ontario and Lake Erie.

The Lowlands

The Great Lakes–St. Lawrence Lowlands are located in southern Ontario. This area contains some of Canada's richest farmland, and most of Ontario's population. From these lowlands rises the Niagara Escarpment, a ridge of limestone that runs northwest from the Niagara River to Manitoulin Island.

Niagara Falls

Over the escarpment cascades one of the world's natural wonders. Niagara Falls is the most powerful waterfall in North America. Goat Island splits it into two sections: the Canadian, or Horseshoe, Falls and the narrower American Falls.

The waters of the Niagara River are diverted to produce electricity at the Sir Adam Beck Complex – one of Ontario's largest hydroelectric power plants.

Every minute, 155 million litres of water rush over the Horseshoe Falls.

The Canadian Shield

One of Ontario's most incredible natural features is in the north. The Canadian Shield is a large, horseshoe-shaped basin of rock. It is so large that it extends into five other provinces and two territories.

The Canadian Shield includes forests and thousands of lakes, rivers and streams.

The rocky Canadian Shield landscape is dotted with lakes, rivers and forests. The rock is rich in mineral ores such as iron, platinum, gold and nickel.

There are many small lakes on the Canadian Shield. Some, called kettle lakes, were formed after the last ice age. Retreating glaciers left chunks of ice embedded in sediment. These melted into small, deep, kettle-shaped lakes.

Trees, trees and more trees

Ontario has about 70 million hectares of forest. There are four forest regions. The Hudson Bay Lowlands are an area of **barrens** south of Hudson and James Bays.

They contain meadows, a type of bog called **muskeg** and all of Ontario's **tundra**.

The boreal forest is below the Hudson Bay Lowlands and is the largest forest region in the province. Here, the spruce, pine, cedar and balsam forests are home to many animals, including moose, caribou, black bears and wolves.

Hudson Bay Lowlands muskeg

Black bears live in Ontario's boreal forest.

The Great Lakes-St. Lawrence forest extends along the St. Lawrence River across central Ontario to Lakes Huron and Superior. It contains a mix of coniferous, or evergreen, trees and **deciduous** trees.

The deciduous forest is Ontario's southernmost forest. It is located north of lakes Ontario and Erie. It has many rare plant and animal species, including the southern flying squirrel. Much of the forest has been cleared for farms and cities.

Southern flying squirrels (above) live in Ontario's deciduous forests, where autumn is a riot of colour.

Hot and cold!

A summer day in southern Ontario can reach a sticky 34 degrees Celsius, but the moist air can make it feel ten degrees hotter! Summers are more comfortable and drier in northern areas.

Most of Ontario receives 500 or more millimetres of rain a year. This is excellent for growing crops. Ontario winters can be almost snowless in parts of the southwest, but several metres of snow fall in the north and in the province's snow belts. Here more than three metres of snow can fall each year!

Fascinating Ontario facts

- You can't live any farther south in Canada than Point Pelee and Pelee Island in Lake Erie. They are on the same latitude as northern California. Each September, thousands of monarch butterflies cluster on the trees here before continuing on their annual migration to Mexico.

- The eastern massasauga rattlesnake is Ontario's only venomous snake. Its territory is in southern and central Ontario.

- Manitoulin Island in Lake Huron is the largest freshwater island in the world. It is so large that it includes the largest lake in a freshwater island in the world – Lake Manitou.

Archaeologists examine an Aboriginal burial ground revealed during construction. Local First Nations peoples held a ceremony to rebury the remains.

Chapter 2
The Living Past

Ontario became a province of Canada at **Confederation** in 1867, but long before that many people had lived and settled in the area. The first residents were Algonkian- and Iroquoian-speaking peoples. Their history goes back more than 10,000 years. The Algonkian-speaking peoples, including the Cree, Ojibwa, Algonquin and Mississauga, lived in the north and east.

The Iroquoian-
speaking peoples,
including the Huron,
Tobacco, Erie and
Iroquois, lived in the
north, east and south.

The Aboriginal peoples lived off the land.
They fished and hunted elk, caribou, moose
and deer. Some were also farmers, growing
corn, beans and squash. Today, about 190,000
descendants of Ontario's first peoples live in
the province, many on reserves, or land set
aside for them.

The first Europeans

French explorer Étienne Brûlé was the first European to explore parts of what is now Ontario. The French had already established a fur trade in **New France**. To expand the fur trade, Brûlé was sent west in 1610 to trade with the Aboriginal peoples.

The British also began trading in furs in their North American colonies to the south. Both the French and British went on to set up fur trading posts throughout the area that today is Ontario. They battled over control of the land and the fur trade for many years.

Artist Frances Anne Hopkins travelled several times with her husband, a Hudson's Bay Company official, on his tours. Her 1869 painting, *Canoe Manned by Voyageurs Passing a Waterfall*, is believed to be of the French River.

The fur trade

How could the skins of beavers trigger exploration, discovery and wars? For 300 years, from the 1500s to the early 1800s, the fur trade was the most important industry in North America. Beaver pelts were shipped to Europe where they were made into fashionable hats. France and Britain constantly competed for fur trade territory. Their explorers and traders mapped the land and set up trading posts in places that would later become major North American cities.

The Loyalists arrive

Some of the most prominent early settlers to Ontario were the United Empire Loyalists. They came as a result of the **American Revolution** (1775-1783). The British were defeated during the revolution and the United States of America was formed. The **colonists** who had remained loyal to the British left their homes and came north to areas still under British control. They were given land to settle on.

The many names of Ontario

Ontario has had many different names over the years. For a time, it was part of French-controlled territory and referred to as *le pays d'en haut*. After the **Seven Years War** ended in 1763, France lost its North American territory to the British. In 1791 Ontario was called Upper Canada. By 1841 Upper Canada became known as Canada West. Finally, Canada West was renamed Ontario at Confederation in 1867.

Joseph Brant, or Thayendanegea, was a Mohawk leader who fought with the British during the American Revolution. For his loyalty, he and his followers were granted land in British territory. The land became the Six Nations reserve near Brantford, Ontario.

North to freedom!

In 1793 the first lieutenant-governor of Upper Canada, John Graves Simcoe, passed an anti-slavery act. This helped make Upper Canada a refuge for escaped slaves from the United States. From 1800 to 1865, about 20,000 people fled slavery in America and came to Ontario. They used a network called the **Underground Railroad**. Many settled in southern Ontario. Their descendants still live here today.

Josiah Henson, an escaped slave, founded a settlement and school for former slaves near Dresden, Ontario.

British General Isaac Brock was killed at the Battle of Queenston Heights. It was one of many famous War of 1812 battles.

The War of 1812

By 1812 about 80,000 people were living in Upper Canada. Across the Atlantic Ocean, Britain and France were at war again. When the British stopped American ships from trading with France, the Americans became angry and entered the war against Britain and its colonies. Over the next two years, the British army and local **militias** fought off several American invasions. In the end, Canada was safe.

Rebellion

Upper Canada was the scene of a famous rebellion in 1837. The rebels were farmers and business people who were upset by a government called the Family Compact, which granted favours to friends and relatives. A rebellion at the same time in Lower Canada led Britain to unite Upper and Lower Canada in 1841 into the province of Canada: Canada West (Ontario) and Canada East (Quebec).

Rebels armed with guns and pikes march down Yonge Street toward Toronto. The rebellion was put down.

Sir John A. Macdonald was elected Canada's first prime minister in 1867. Macdonald's family came to Canada from Scotland and settled in Kingston, Ontario.

Railways and factories

Canada West continued to grow. Railways, roads and canals were built to bring trade goods and people across the land. The new forms of transportation brought wealth to cities. The age of manufacturing began. By the time Canada West became the province of Ontario at Confederation, it was a strong political and economic force in the country.

Niagara Falls, Ontario, like many other communities, celebrates Canada Day on July 1 with fireworks. On July 1, 1867, New Brunswick, Nova Scotia, Canada West (Ontario) and Canada East (Quebec) joined to become the country of Canada.

Steel factories in Hamilton, Ontario, attracted immigrant workers in the early 1900s.

A growing province

Ontario continued to grow after Confederation. By the early 1900s, more people were living in cities than on farms. New industries began to develop, including mining, textiles, and the making of steel and automobiles. These industries attracted immigrant workers, at first from western and eastern Europe. Later immigrants came from Asia, the Caribbean and Africa. Most immigrants settled in the cities of southern Ontario, including Toronto, Ottawa, Hamilton and London, creating lively multicultural centres.

Chapter 3
Wilderness and City

Eighty-five per cent of Ontario's population lives in the south, close to the Great Lakes and the American border. The idea of a wilderness getaway is strong in Ontario. In the summer, many Ontarians spend their leisure time swimming, fishing and boating on lakes.

Some have cottages in central or northern Ontario. Highways heading north are often clogged with cottage-goers on summer weekends. The province has 5 national parks and 329 provincial parks. Most of them are located by a lake.

Nature and art

Many early paintings of Ontario depict a wilderness of trees, rock and water. Artist Tom Thomson loved to paint northern Ontario. His bold landscapes influenced the Group of Seven. They used broad brushstrokes and great globs of paint to portray the Canadian outdoors.

Thomson conveyed the beauty of Ontario's world-famous Algonquin Provincial Park in *The West Wind*.

Tom Thomson, *The West Wind*, winter 1916–1917

Writing about "the bush"

"I was perfectly bewildered – I could only stare at the place, with my eyes swimming in tears," wrote Susanna Moodie about coming to Ontario – a strange, new land – in the 1830s.

Susanna and her sister Catharine Parr Traill were among Canada's first authors. These two gentlewomen emigrated from England in 1832 with their husbands and settled in the wilderness north of Peterborough.

It wasn't easy. Their letters and books, especially *Roughing It in the Bush* and *The Backwoods of Canada*, describe a life very different from what they left in England, including clearing the land and gathering for barn-building bees.

Susanna Moodie (top) and Catharine Parr Traill were also artists. Susanna painted this watercolour, *Goldfinch and Thistle*.

Cities of culture

When Ontarians aren't enjoying the great outdoors, they are off to concerts, plays and festivals.

One of Ontario's most famous theatrical events is the Stratford Shakespeare Festival. It showcases plays by English playwright William Shakespeare, who lived in the 1600s. The festival began in a tent in the 1950s. Today it is one of the most respected theatre companies in North America.

From spring to fall, visitors to Stratford come to see plays performed on the Festival Theatre's unique apron stage.

Ottawa, Ontario's second-largest city, is the capital of Canada. Originally a lumber town called Bytown, it is now home to the Parliament Buildings, the National Gallery of Canada and the Canadian War Museum.

The largest museum in Canada – the Royal Ontario Museum – is in Toronto, the capital of the province. One of its exhibits features the biggest dinosaur on display in Canada. The Art Gallery of Ontario is one of the largest art museums in North America. Other museums in Toronto are entirely devoted to shoes, sugar, television – and hockey!

Each winter in Ottawa, part of the Rideau Canal becomes a skating rink 7.8 kilometres long.

The Stanley Cup is North America's oldest professional sports trophy. Though it travels over 200 days a year, its permanent home is at the Hockey Hall of Fame in Toronto.

Singer Avril Lavigne arrives in Toronto for an outdoor music concert. She grew up in Napanee, Ontario.

Based in Toronto, the National Ballet of Canada is the country's largest ballet company. Its school develops skilled dancers who go on to perform all over the world.

Toronto is Canada's largest city, with a population of 2.5 million. Here the CN Tower, the second-tallest free-standing structure in the world, rises above the downtown waterfront.

Butter tarts and sweet corn

Mmm…butter tarts! The pastry filled with a gooey mixture of butter, sugar, eggs and sometimes raisins and nuts has been a tradition in northern Ontario for over 100 years. Many Ontario treats have their origin in farm kitchens, where hearty foods made with rich butter, cream and fat were whipped up as midday meals for hungry farm workers.

Sweet corn, eaten on the cob, is a summer favourite. But don't bother buying it ahead of time. Folks in southern Ontario farm country like their corn fresh-picked and eaten the same day!

Chapter 4
Made in Ontario

Of all the provinces and territories, Ontario makes the biggest impact on Canada's economy. About 40 per cent of Canada's employment is in Ontario. That's a lot of jobs!

Most of the jobs are in finance, tourism and business services. Mining, forestry and agriculture are also important to Ontario's economy. This is because they contribute to Ontario's largest industry: manufacturing.

Did you know that Ontario produces more than half of all manufactured goods that are shipped out of Canada? More than 90 per cent of them are **exported** to the United States. The province's most important industry is automobile manufacturing. After Michigan, Ontario is the largest producer of automobiles in North America.

Lumber and minerals

Ontario's economy depends on primary industries. These are industries that rely on natural resources. Ontario's immense forest land creates about 90,000 jobs in the timber and pulp and paper industries.

Mining is also big business. The rocks of the Canadian Shield hold a treasure trove of minerals. Ontario is one of the world's top mineral producers. Massive deposits of copper and nickel can be found in the Sudbury Basin in northern Ontario. Most of Ontario's gold mines are in Timmins, Red Lake and Hemlo in the north. Zinc, silver, platinum and cobalt are also mined.

Ontario is the world's second-largest producer of nickel. The northern Ontario city of Sudbury even has a giant nickel that celebrates nickel mining.

Ontario lumber is used in the construction industry.

Down on the farm

Ontario has more than 67,000 farms. Most are located in the south. Farmers grow corn, soybeans, tomatoes and wheat. Fruit such as cherries, peaches and grapes grow near Lake Ontario and Lake Erie. Both the southwestern and central areas of the province are suitable for livestock farming.

Each fall, agricultural fairs are held in farming towns throughout the province. Farmers enter their livestock into competitions where they are judged on how they look or perform. The Royal Agricultural Winter Fair – the largest indoor farm fair in the world – is held each November in Toronto.

Mooove over, we have a winner! A judge chooses a ribbon winner during a Royal Agricultural Winter Fair Holstein competition.

A worker harvests frozen grapes on a cold winter night. The grapes are used for making ice wine, a prized sweet wine for which Ontario is famous.

The largest fruit crop in Ontario is apples. They thrive along the southern shore of Georgian Bay, as well as the northern shores of lakes Ontario and Erie.

Chapter 5
Multiculturalism

Ontario is the country's most culturally diverse province. More than half of Canada's new immigrants settle here and 70 languages, from Mandarin to Urdu, are spoken. You can learn a language at schools and multicultural centres in many cities throughout the province. English classes are available for new immigrants. And every year, colourful festivals celebrate the heritage of the province's people.

A mas-ive celebration

One of these festivals is the Caribbean festival held in Toronto – the country's largest celebration of Caribbean culture. Every August, Toronto bursts with island flavour and style. "Time to show your colours!" the MC yells to the crowd. Thousands of people cheer and dance to the beat of **soca** music. They wave flags from Trinidad and Tobago, Barbados, Jamaica and other parts of the Caribbean.

Hard work is put into costumes of feathers and glitter, some of which tower over 20 metres tall.

Held each summer since 1967, the celebration features competitions for best mas band (masquerade group) and best costume, as well as concerts, steel pan drum shows, a King and Queen dance competition, picnics and a huge parade.

Lederhosen and schnitzel

Gemütlichkeit means friendliness in German, and it's what you'll experience at Oktoberfest! This festival celebrates the German heritage of people who settled in Kitchener and Waterloo almost a century ago. Every October, clubs and halls are transformed with polka music and dancing troupes. More than 70,000 people attend, enjoying traditional German food such as sausage, sauerkraut and wiener schnitzel.

Oktoberfest's mascot is Onkel Hans.

Powwows take place across the province each summer. The Canadian Aboriginal Festival held in Toronto in November is the largest festival of Aboriginal culture in Canada.

Highland Games take place in communities throughout Ontario that have a strong history of Scottish settlement, including Maxville, Chatham, Fergus and Hamilton.

Chapter 6
Points of Pride

▶ Frederick Banting and Charles Best won the Nobel Prize for Medicine in 1923 for developing insulin in a Toronto laboratory. Insulin is a drug that helps people with **diabetes** stay alive.

▶ The first long-distance telephone call was made in Ontario! On August 3, 1876, Alexander Graham Bell called from Brantford to Mount Pleasant, a distance of six kilometres.

▶ The longest street in the world is in Ontario! Yonge Street runs 1896 kilometres from downtown Toronto through central and northern Ontario to Rainy River on the Ontario-Minnesota border.

▶ Born and raised in Brantford, Wayne Gretzky has been called the greatest hockey player of all time. As a child, Gretzky honed his skills on a backyard rink. He went on to dazzle in junior hockey and break records in the National Hockey League.

▶ Mike Lazaridis of Waterloo, Ontario, co-founded Research In Motion (RIM), one of Canada's most successful high-tech companies. RIM developed the BlackBerry, a wireless phone, email, text-messaging and web-browsing device. Millions of people own BlackBerrys.

▶ Basketball was invented by James Naismith, who grew up near Almonte, Ontario.

Glossary

American Revolution: A war between Britain and its American colonies (1775-1783) by which the colonies won independence and formed the United States of America

barrens: Northern land with sandy soil and few trees

colonists: People who leave their country to settle in a new land

Confederation: The joining of Ontario, Quebec, New Brunswick and Nova Scotia into the Dominion of Canada in 1867

deciduous: Describes trees and bushes that shed their leaves in autumn

descendants: People whose background can be traced to a certain group or person

diabetes: A disease in which the body cannot control the level of sugar in the blood

ethnic: Describes a shared culture and language

exported: Sent to another country for trade

militias: Groups of citizens who are not professional soldiers but who serve in times of war

muskeg: A mossy swamp

New France: French colonies or land in North America before 1763

Seven Years War: A European war (1756-1763) involving England, France and their allies that spilled over into North America. At the end of the war, France lost its colonies in North America.

soca: A type of lively Caribbean music

tundra: A treeless arctic plain

Underground Railroad: A system that helped runaway slaves from the southern United States escape to Canada or safe northern states